Goodnight Morrígan

by Hannah Storyteller and Morpheus Ravenna

Text copyright © 2019 Mousagetes Books
Images copyright © 2019 Morpheus Ravenna
ISBN 9780578441948

Goodnight Morrígan

On the great battlefield
There was a mighty Queen

Our enemies' bane,
And the keeper of -

The Morrígan is a complex goddess who is sometimes understood as a collective. She often appears as one of three.

Restless souls of the slain

And there were two little crows
feasting on foes

If you like this illustration, you may enjoy the traditional Scottish ballad "The Twa Corbies."

And three vigilant ravens
Watching over safe havens

And a bright wall of swords
All be-spelled as wards

Many ancient Celtic peoples believed that weapons could have spirits within them, with oracular and protective powers.

And a druid and a healing brew
and a curious dog too

And a drunken warrior shouting
"abú!"

The druids were priests among early Celtic peoples, with knowledge of healing arts, poetry, magic, and ritual.

Goodnight Morrígan.

Goodnight bloody campaign
Goodnight restless souls of
the slain

While the Morrígan isn't a psychopomp per se, she is associated with the restless dead and is said to haunt battlefields.

Goodnight Great Queen
And our enemies' bane

The name "Morrígan" is usually translated as Great Queen but can also be understood to mean Phantom Queen.

Goodnight crows
Goodnight foes

The Morrígan is associated with several kinds of corvids, including the ravens, the carrion crow, and especially the hooded crow.

Goodnight ravens
And goodnight safe havens

The fort depicted here is inspired by early medieval ring forts in Ireland.

Goodnight shields
And goodnight battlefields

The armor, shields and weapons on this page are inspired by those from many different places and time periods: some are Gallic in style while others are Irish, Norse, or Anglo-Saxon.

Goodnight swords
And goodnight wards

A ward is a term for a protective magical charm. Many Celtic customs attribute protective magic to blades, especially those that contain iron.

Goodnight druids
Goodnight healing brew

Cauldrons or wells with the power to heal the wounded feature in several stories from Irish and Welsh mythology.

Goodnight cave
Goodnight Cú

The Cave of Cats (Úaimh na gCait in Irish) is the home of the Morrígan and traditionally was a place for warriors to be tested, including the legendary warrior Cú Chulain, whose name means Culann's Hound.

Goodnight drunken warriors
Shouting "Abú!"

"Abú!" is a historical Irish war cry that can still sometimes be heard at sporting events.

Goodnight Queen
Goodnight comrades fair
Goodnight warriors everywhere

About the Morrígan

The Morrígan is most well known as an Irish battle goddess who often appears in crow or raven form, and is associated with warriors, sovereignty, prophecy, and the power of the Otherworld. We meet the Morrígan in early medieval Irish literature, as well as finding her in folklore old and new. She is closely related to war goddesses known and worshiped in the ancient Celtic cultures of Britain and Gaul as well.

The Irish myths featuring the Morrígan reflect early medieval perceptions of Iron Age Celtic society, a cattle-raiding warrior culture, and in these stories she is often shown as a goddess of battle, warriors, and the dead. The Morrígan is deeply associated with incitement of heroes toward glory in battle, with the granting of victory, and with their deaths. She also fulfills an important role as a poetess and prophetess.

To learn more about the Morrígan, here are some sources for further reading:

Daimler, Morgan. 2014. Pagan Portals – The Morrigan: Meeting the Great Queens. Moon Books.
Epstein, Angelique Gulermovich. 1998. War Goddess: The Morrígan and Her Germano-Celtic Counterparts. University of California.
Ravenna, Morpheus. 2015. The Book of The Great Queen: The Many Faces of the Morrigan from Ancient Legends to Modern Devotions. Concrescent Press.

Coru Cathubodua Priesthood resources. http://www.corupriesthood.com/spirituality/resources/
Lora O'Brien: Irish author, guide, and priest of the Morrígan. https://loraobrien.ie/
Story Archaeology: Irish mythology podcast and blog. https://storyarchaeology.com/

About the Authors

Morpheus Ravenna is a spiritual worker, artist, and writer. A tattoo artist and illustrator by trade, she also practices and teaches devotional polytheism and the magical arts. Her primary spiritual practice is her devotion and dedication to the Morrígan within the framework of Celtic heroic spirituality, and she is a co-founder of the Coru Cathubodua Priesthood. Author of The Book of the Great Queen: The Many Faces of the Morrígan from Ancient Legends to Modern Devotions, her writing can also be found on her personal blog, The Shieldmaiden. She also practices medieval armored combat and is very fond of spears.

She can be reached through her website at www.bansheearts.com.

Hannah Storyteller is a bard who writes and tells new stories about old gods. She is a devotional polytheist, a self-defense instructor, an artisan, and an alleged werewolf. Her primary spiritual practice consists of shouting "ward your rituals!" at anyone who will listen and a great many people who will not.

More of her pagan children's books for adults can be found at www.mousagetesbooks.com

CPSIA information can be obtained at www.ICGtesting.com
Printed in the USA
LVIW010743040319
609385LV00004B/37